GREAT MINDS® WIT & WISDOM™

Grade 8 Module 1:
The Poetics and Power of Storytelling

Student Edition

COPYRIGHT STATEMENT

Published by Great Minds®.

Copyright ©2016 Great Minds®. All rights reserved. No part of this work may be reproduced or used in any form or by any means—graphic, electronic, or mechanical, including photocopying or information storage and retrieval systems—without written permission from the copyright holder.

978-1-68386-049-5

Table of Contents

GRADE 8 MODULE 1

Lesson Handouts

Handout 1A: Fluency Homework

Handout 1B: Relationship Maps

Handout 5A: Character Relationships

Handout 6A: Poem Frame

Handout 8A: Vertical and Horizontal Images in "Dear Jordan"

Handout 11A: Frayer Model

Handout 12A: Narrative Arc in "Third Quarter"

Handout 13A: Write Like—Occasional Poem

Handout 14A: "Free Throws" Paragraph

Handout 15A: Evidence Collection for *Crossover*

Handout 16A: Collect Evidence—Form and Meaning in *The Crossover*

Handout 16B: Frayer Model

Handout 19A: Poetic Performance and Reading Analysis

Handout 20A: Evidence Collection

Handout 21A: Poetry Performance Checklist

Handout 23A: Summarizing "Your Brain on Fiction"

Handout 24A: An Excerpt from "The Man Made of Words"

Handout 25A: Five Important Words from "The Man Made of Words"

Handout 25B Incorporating Textual Evidence

Handout 27A: Evidence Collection

Handout 28A: Identify and Revise Sentence Structure

Handout 29A: EOM Portfolio Planning Packet

Handout 29B EOM Exemplar Poems

Handout 30A: EOM Exemplar Cover Letter

Handout 30B: Drafting Cover Letter Paragraphs

Handout 30C: Narrative Writing Checklist

Volume of Reading Reflection Questions

Wit & Wisdom Parent Tip Sheet

Copyright © 2016 Great Minds®

Handout 1A: Fluency Homework

Directions:
1. Day 1: Read the text carefully and annotate to help you read fluently.
2. Each day:
    a. Practice reading the text three to five times.
    b. Evaluate your progress by placing a ✔+, ✔, or ✔- in each unshaded box.
    c. Ask someone (adult or peer) to listen and evaluate you as well.
3. Last day: Respond to the self-reflection questions at the end of this handout.

Poem title: _____

Page numbers: _____

Student Performance Checklist:	Day 1		Day 2		Day 3		Day 4	
	You	Listener*	You	Listener*	You	Listener*	You	Listener*
Accurately read the passage 3–5 times.								
Read with appropriate phrasing and pausing.								
Read with appropriate expression.								
Read articulately at a good pace and an audible volume.								

Self-reflection: What choices did you make when deciding how to read this passage, and why? What would you like to improve on or try differently next time? (*Thoughtfully answer these questions on the back of this paper.*)

*Adult or peer

Name

Date **Class**

Handout 1B: Relationship Maps

PART 1: Review the examples.

Directions: *Words represent ideas that can have many different relationships. Some of the relationships are listed below:*

1. Synonyms
2. Antonyms
3. Parts of a whole
4. Cause and effect
5. Items in a category
6. Steps in a sequence
7. Description of an object

You can visually represent these relationships:

Parts of a whole	Steps in a sequence or Cause and effect

PART 2: Complete a Relationship Map.

Directions: *On the back of this handout, draw a relationship map that represents the relationship between* storytelling, power, content *and* form. *You may also use key words from the definitions to make your relationship map.*

Name

Date   Class

Handout 5A: Character Relationships

PART A: "Dad Takes Us to Krispy Kreme and Tells Us His Favorite Story (Again)"

Directions: *Reread "Dad Takes Us to Krispy Kreme and Tells Us His Favorite Story (Again)" (page 63), and answer the following questions before returning to your home group.*

1. What do the title and the first four lines of this poem reveal about the twins' relationship to their father?

2. What is the effect of Chuck's analogy about the twins' first basketball shot?

3. What is the message about expectations in this poem?

4. Choose one example from the poem, and explain what it reveals about the characters' relationships.

PART B: "Mom Shouts"

Directions: *Reread "Mom Shouts" (page 74), and answer the following questions before returning to your home group.*

1. Why does Crystal tell Chuck "this isn't a basketball game"?

2. What do Chuck's reactions reveal about the relationship between Josh's parents?

3. How does Josh's eavesdropping deepen your understanding of the Bell family?

PART C: "Gym Class"

Directions: Reread "Gym Class" (page 84), and answer the following questions before returning to your home group.

1. How do the changes in gym class relate to Josh's relationship with JB?

2. Why does Josh believe this situation is "unfair"?

3. In addition to being a CPR/first-aid tool, what might the "dummy" represent, or symbolize, in the poem?

Handout 6A: Poem Frame

Directions: Complete the poem frame below using descriptive and sensory language. Consult a thesaurus to help you generate effective word choices. Remember to title the poem!

"_____"

Josh Bell is a real cool and _____ guy [precise adjective]

He plays basketball like _____, so fly [simile]

Every time he's on the court the crowd _____ [active verb]

Seriously, Josh is _____, I wouldn't lie! [metaphor]

His old man's real _____, too. [precise adjective]

He has a twin named JB, who is _____, [metaphor]

But lately Josh is feeling like _____, [simile]

What is there for Josh, aka Filthy McNasty, to do?

Handout 8A: Vertical and Horizontal Images in "Dear Jordan"

Directions: Read and explain the vertical and horizontal images from "Dear Jordan," and write a new image has a similar meaning.

Image from a vertical read	Image from a horizontal read	Explanation	New image

without u
 	
the goal
 	
seems
 	
broken
	without u
	          i am empty,
	the goal
	          with no net.		

like puzzle pieces
 	
i can no longer fit
	Seems
	          my life was
	broken
	          shattered,
	like puzzle pieces
	          on the court.
	i can no longer fit.		

can you run with me,	like two brothers		
like we used to?	burning up		
Stealing sun,	together		
burning up.			

Image from a vertical read	Image from a horizontal read	Explanation	New image
help me heal, slash with me like two stars like two brothers together.	can you help me heal, run with me, slash with me like we used to? like two stars stealing sun		

Handout 11A: Frayer Model

PART A:
Directions: *Complete the Frayer Model for the word you've chosen from* The Crossover.

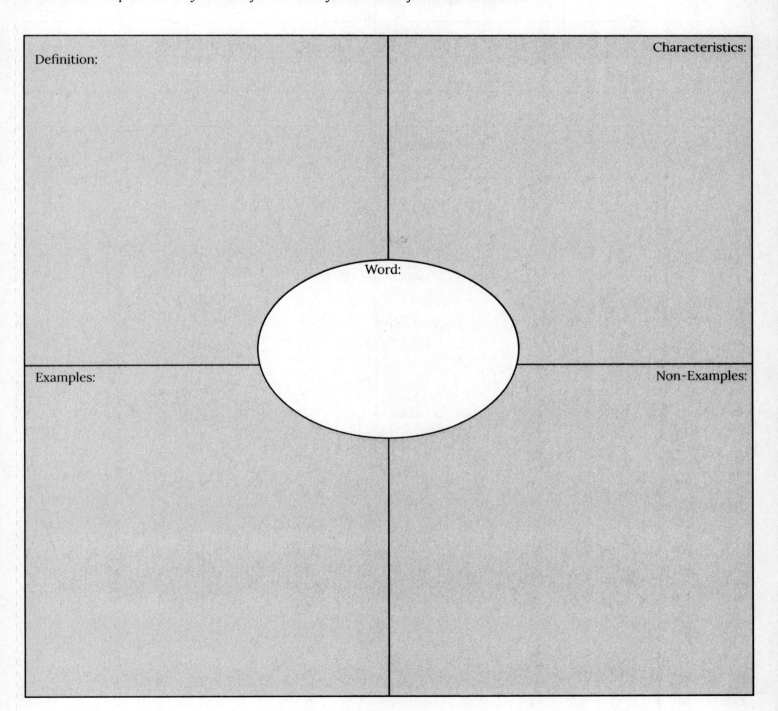

Name

Date   Class

PART B:

Directions: *Return to the poem that includes this word. How has your understanding of the sentence and poem changed now that you know more about this word?*

_____

_____

_____

_____

Handout 12A: Narrative Arc in "Third Quarter"

Directions: *Respond to the following questions to complete an analysis of structure and narrative arc in the "Third Quarter" section of* The Crossover.

---

1. Twice in this article the importance of having a "coherent" story is emphasized. What does *coherent* mean, and why is coherence important for a story?

---

2. In sequence, list the major events in "Third Quarter" that define the story of this section.

-
-
-

Stage of Narrative Arc Poem	What is happening in this poem?	How does the poem contribute to the narrative arc of "Third Quarter"?
Beginning "After" (Alexander 137)		
Middle "I run into Dad's room" (165–167)		
End "At Noon, in the Gym, with Dad" (194–196)		

3. Which poem is most important in this narrative arc? Why?

Handout 13A: Write Like–Occasional Poem

Directions: *On this occasion of completing your reading of* The Crossover, *you will write a poem, called* **"Teacher, since you asked, I'll tell you about my reading of The Crossover."**

Express how you feel and what you think now that you have finishing your reading of this novel-in-verse. What are your responses to the story? What moments, images, or interactions stick with you (for good or bad)? What surprised, angered, or excited you? What questions do you still have? What questions did you have that have been answered?

As you compose your free-verse poem, include narrative elements we have practiced together, including:

- Descriptive and sensory language
- Metaphor and simile
- Verb moods
- Sentence variation

Consider including repetition or rhythm.

- Example of repetition: the use of Because as the start of each line in "Mom, since you asked, I'll tell you why I'm so angry."
- You might extend the repetition: "I used to think _____. But now I know _____."
  OR: "I used to feel that _____. But now I feel that _____."
- Example of rhythm: the two-word lines in "At Noon, in the Gym, with Dad" (194–196).

Focus on writing in your personal voice. What language, tone, and style best represent you?

My Occasional Poem:

"Teacher, since you asked, I'll tell you about my reading of *The Crossover*"

Handout 14A: "Free Throws" Paragraph

Directions: Use the following organizer to complete an analysis of the poem "Free Throws."

Topic Statement (state your essential idea about a topic): "Free Throws" develops the meaning of the story because _____ and _____.	
Evidence (cite evidence that develops your topic, including necessary content): The poem shows _____ because _____.	**Elaboration** (explain how the evidence develops your topic): This develops the story's meaning because _____.
Evidence: The free throw can also be interpreted as a symbol that distills the story's meaning because _____.	**Elaboration** (develop your point with a specific example from the poem): _____.
Concluding Statement (reinforce your essential idea): "Free Throws" is a fitting end to *The Crossover* because _____ _____.	

Handout 15A: Evidence Collection for *Crossover*

Directions: *Consider the use of the word crossover—or a variation of the word—in each of the following instances.*

Text	What does the word mean in this context? • Use a dictionary when necessary. • Record connotations. • Is the word used in a figurative sense? A literal sense? Both?
The title, *The Crossover*	
"cross o ver" (29)	
"Article #2 in the Daily News (January 14)" (225–226)	
"Where Do We Go from Here?" (227–228)	
"Free Throws" (234–237)	

Explain how the meaning of the word crossover changes over the course of the novel by describing the different uses of the word crossover in terms of a narrative arc.

Which use of the word represents the meaning of the beginning of the story? Why?

Which use of the word represents the meaning of the middle of the story? Why?

Which use of the word represents the meaning of the end of the story? Why?

Name _____

Date _____ Class _____

Handout 16A: Collect Evidence—Form and Meaning in *The Crossover*

Directions: Choose two poetic types from the Poetic Types anchor chart that you feel most contribute to the overall meaning of *The Crossover*. Then identify an example of each type in the novel that exemplifies this contribution to the novel's meaning.

	Poetic Type: **Poem:**	**Poetic Type:** **Poem:**
What is happening in this poem?		
What are the elements that structure the poem? • Characteristics of poetic type • Rhyme/rhythm/repetition • Line breaks/stanzas		
How do specific language choices, lines, and incidents in the poem develop your understanding of Josh Bell's sense of self?		
How do specific language choices, lines, and incidents in the poem develop your understanding of Josh Bell's sense of his world?		
How does the structure of this poem convey how stories help Josh make sense of himself or the world around him?		

Handout 16B: Frayer Model

Complete the Frayer Model for irony *and* ironic.

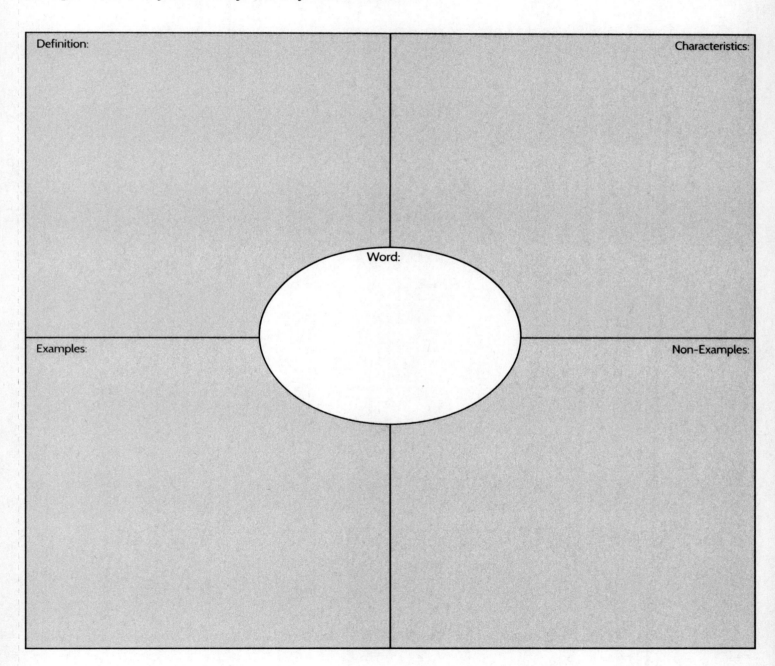

Name _____

Date _____ Class _____

Handout 19A: Poetic Performance and Reading Analysis

Directions: Respond to questions about the poem and performance of "Nikki-Rosa" by Nikki Giovanni or "Slam, Dunk, and Hook" by Yusef Komunyakaa.

Poem Title:

By:

1. Summarize: What is the poem about? What story is being told?

2. Choose the <u>most</u> <u>important</u> line from this poem and paraphrase the meaning of that line.

Original Line:

Paraphrase:

3. Explain how the chosen line contributes to the overall meaning of the poem, and why you identified it as most important.

Name

Date   Class

4. Describe the performance or reading of this poem in your own words. Who is the audience? What choices is this poet making about how to express their poem orally?

Name _____

Date _____ Class _____

Handout 20A: Evidence Collection

Directions: *Respond to questions about each of the poetry performances in this module.*

Text	Who is the audience for this performance?	How does the audience shape the choices the poet makes in performing?

Name _____

Date _____ Class _____

Handout 21A: Poetry Performance Checklist

Directions: *Respond to questions about each of the poetry performances in this module.*

Poetry Performance Checklist			
	Self +/ Δ	Peer +/ Δ	Teacher +/ Δ
I used varied volume and appropriate emphasis.			
I paused for emphasis at least once.			
I read at an appropriate pace, varying speed appropriate to the content of my poem.			
I changed my inflection to indicate a variety of punctuation as needed.			
I used a tone appropriate to the content of my poem.			
I made at least one gesture appropriate to the content of my poem.			
I considered the identity of my audience when making decisions about my performance.			
I engaged with my audience.			
Total # of checks			

Name _____

Date _____ Class _____

Handout 23A: Summarizing "Your Brain on Fiction"

Directions: *Provide the central idea, supporting ideas, and a brief account of how these ideas develop in "Your Brain on Fiction."*

Central Idea:

- Supporting idea:
- Supporting idea:
- Supporting idea:

How does the author use the supporting ideas to develop the central idea over the course of the text?

Summary:

Handout 24A: An Excerpt from "The Man Made of Words"

Directions: Read the following excerpt from a lecture given by N. Scott Momaday, published as an essay in 1998; use your Glossary to define any unfamiliar vocabulary words.

The following excerpt is from a lecture given by N. Scott Momaday, published as an essay in 1998.

I want to try to put several different ideas together this morning. And in the process, I hope to **indicate** something about the nature of the relationship between language and experience. It seems to me that in a certain sense we are all made of words; that our most essential being **consists** in language. It is the element in which we think and dream and act, in which we live our daily lives. There is no way in which we can exist apart from the **morality** of a verbal **dimension**.

In one of the discussions yesterday the question "What is an American Indian?" was raised.

The answer of course is that an Indian is an idea which a given man has of himself. And it is a **moral** idea, for it accounts for the way in which he reacts to other men and to the world in general. And that idea, in order to be realized completely, has to be expressed.

I want to say some things then about this moral and verbal **dimension** in which we live. I want to say something about such things as **ecology** and storytelling and the imagination. Let me tell you a story:

One night a strange thing happened. I had written the greater part of *The Way to Rainy Mountain*—all of it, in fact, except the epilogue. I had set down the last of the old **Kiowa** tales, and I had composed both the historical and the autobiographical commentaries for it. I had the sense of being out of breath, of having said what it was in me to say on that subject. The manuscript lay before me in the bright light. Small, to be sure, but complete, or nearly so. I had written the second of the two poems in which that book is framed. I had uttered the last word, as it were. And yet a whole, **penultimate** piece was missing. I began once again to write.

During the first hours after midnight on the morning of November 13, 1833, it seemed that the world was coming to an end. Suddenly the stillness of the night was broken; there were brilliant flashes of light in the sky, light of such intensity that people were awakened by it. With the speed and density of a driving rain, stars were falling in the universe. Some were brighter than Venus; one was said to be as large as the moon. I went on to say that that event, the falling of the stars on North America, that explosion of meteors which occurred 137 years ago, is among the earliest entries in the Kiowa calendars. So deeply impressed upon the imagination of the Kiowas is that old **phenomenon** that it is remembered still; it has become a part of the racial memory.

"The living memory," I wrote, "and the verbal tradition which **transcends** it, were brought together for me once and for all in the person of Ko-sahn." It seemed eminently right for me to deal, after all, with that old woman. Ko-sahn is among the most **venerable** people I have ever known. She spoke and sang to me one summer afternoon in Oklahoma. It was like a dream. When I was born she was already old; she was a grown woman when my grandparents came into the world. She sat perfectly still, folded over on herself. It did not seem possible that so many years—a century of years—could be so **compacted** and **distilled**. Her voice shuddered, but it did not fail. Her songs were sad. An old whimsy, a delight in language and in remembrance, shone in her one good eye. She **conjured** up the past, imagining perfectly the long **continuity** of her being. She imagined the lovely young girl, wild and vital, she had been. She imagined the Sun Dance:

There was an old, old woman. She had something on her back. The boys went out to see. The old woman had a bag full of earth on her back. It was a certain kind of sandy earth. That is what they must have in the lodge. The dancers must dance upon the sandy earth. The old woman held a digging tool in her hand. She turned towards the south and pointed with her lips. It was like a kiss, and she began to sing:

We have brought the earth.
Now it is time to play.

As old as I am, I still have the feeling of play. That was the beginning of the Sun Dance.

By this time I was back into the book, caught up completely in the act of writing. I had projected myself—imagined myself—out of the room and out of time. I was there with Ko-sahn in the Oklahoma July. We laughed easily together; I felt that I had known her all of my life—all of hers. I did not want to let her go. But I had come to the end. I set down, almost **grudgingly**, the last sentences:

It was—all of this and more—a **quest**, a going forth upon the way of Rainy Mountain. Probably Ko-sahn too is dead now. At times, in the quiet of evening, I think she must have wondered, dreaming, who she was. Was she become in her sleep that old **purveyor** of the sacred earth, perhaps, that ancient one who, old as she was, still had the feeling of play? And in her mind, at times, did she see the falling stars?

For some time I sat looking down at these words on the page, trying to deal with the emptiness that had come about inside of me. The words did not seem real. I could scarcely believe that they made sense, that they had anything whatsoever to do with meaning. In desperation almost, I went back over the final paragraphs, backwards and forwards, hurriedly. My eyes fell upon the name Ko-sahn. And all at once everything seemed suddenly to refer to that name. The name seemed to **humanize** the whole complexity of language. All at once, absolutely, I had the sense of the magic of words and of names. Ko-sahn, I said, and I said again KO-SAHN.

Then it was that that ancient, one-eyed woman Ko-sahn stepped out of the language and stood before me on the page. I was amazed. Yet it seemed entirely appropriate that this should happen.

"I was just now writing about you," I replied, **stammering**. "I thought—forgive me—I thought that perhaps you were…that you had…"

"No," she said. And she **cackled**, I thought. And she went on. "You have imagined me well, and so I am. You have imagined that I dream, and so I do. I have seen the falling stars."

"But all of this, this imagining," I protested, "this has taken place—is taking place in my mind. You are not actually here, not here in this room." It occurred to me that I was being extremely rude, but I could not help myself. She seemed to understand.

"Be careful of your **pronouncements**, grandson," she answered. "You imagine that I am here in this room, do you not? That is worth something. You see, I have existence, whole being, in your imagination. It is but one kind of being, to be sure, but it is perhaps the best of all kinds. If I am not here in this room, grandson, then surely neither are you."

"I think I see what you mean," I said meekly. I felt justly **rebuked**. "Tell me, grandmother, how old are you?"

"I do not know," she replied. "There are times when I think that I am the oldest woman on earth. You know, the Kiowas came into the world through a hollow log. In my mind's eye I have seen them emerge, one by one, from the mouth of the log. I have seen them so clearly, how they were dressed, how delighted they were to see the world around them. I must have been there. And I must have taken part in that old migration of the Kiowas from Yellowstone to the Southern Plains, near the Big Horn River, and I have seen the red cliffs of Palo Duro Canyon. I was with those who were camped in the Wichita Mountains when the stars fell."

"You are indeed very old," I said, "and you have seen many things."

"Yes, I imagine that I have," she replied. Then she turned slowly around, nodding once, and **receded** into the language I had made. And then I imagined I was alone in the room.

[…]

But let me get back to the matter of storytelling.

I must have taken part in that old migration of the Kiowas from the Yellowstone to the Southern Plains, for I have seen **antelope** bounding in the tall grass near the Big Horn River, and I have seen the ghost forests in the Black Hills. Once I saw the red cliffs of Palo Duro Canyon. I was with those who were camped in the Wichita Mountains when the stars fell. "You are very old," I said, "and you have seen many things." "Yes, I imagined that I have," she replied. Then she turned slowly around, nodding once, and receded into the language I had made. And then I imagine that I was alone in the room.

Who is the storyteller? Of whom is the story told? What is there in the darkness to imagine into being? What is there to dream and to **relate**? What happens when I or anyone **exerts** the force of language upon the unknown?

These are the questions which interest me most.

If there is any absolute assumption in the back of my thoughts tonight, it is this: We are what we imagine. Our very existence consists in our imagination of ourselves. Our best destiny is to imagine, at least, completely, who and what, and *that* we are. The greatest tragedy that can befall us is to go unimagined.

Momaday, N. Scott. "The Man Made of Words." *Nothing But the Truth: An Anthology of Native American Literature*, edited by John Purdy and James Ruppert, Prentice Hall, 2001, pp. 82-95.

Name _____

Date _____   Class _____

Handout 25A: Five Important Words from "The Man Made of Words"

Directions: Decide on five words from "The Man Made of Words" that are most essential to understanding the essay's central idea. First define your word. Then write briefly about why this word is important to your understanding of the essay. Finally, use the word in a sentence.

Word	Definition	Why is it important?	Use it in a sentence
1.			
2.			
3.			
4.			
5.			

Name _____

Date _____ Class _____

Handout 25B: Incorporating Textual Evidence

Directions: *Read the following guidelines and complete the sentence stems below.*

Evidence that is well integrated into your writing accomplishes three things:

- It gives your reader text-specific evidence to support your thinking.
- It shows your reader why you are using that particular piece of evidence.
- It adds variation and interest to your writing.

Guidelines

- Choose evidence that is relevant. This means it should strongly support the ideas you want to communicate in your writing.
- Explain <u>why</u> you are including this particular textual evidence. There are many reasons to choose textual evidence, so your job is to make your reason clear to your reader. There are several ways to effectively incorporate evidence:
- Use introductory sentences or phrases to set the scene for your textual evidence.

No Textual Evidence	Incorporates Evidence	Why is this incorporation of evidence effective?
Josh uses figurative language to explain JB's situation on the basketball court. Josh's language is detailed and humorous.	In "Josh's Play by Play," Josh uses figurative language to explain JB's situation on the basketball court. According to Josh, JB is "McDonald's drive-thru open" (131), which adds detail and humor to the poem while developing unique Josh's voice.	

- Provide your own statement to introduce the evidence, followed by a colon.

No Textual Evidence	Incorporates Evidence	Why is this incorporation of evidence effective?
Josh shows he is hurt when his brother JB leaves him for his girlfriend.	Josh shows he is hurt when his brother JB leaves him for his girlfriend, when he states: "you are walking home / by yourself / and your brother owns the world" (115).	

Name _____

Date _____ Class _____

- Use evidence directly in a sentence.

No Textual Evidence	Incorporates Evidence	Why is this incorporation of evidence effective?
Despite using hyperbolic words, Josh's definition poem on page 154 accurately describes his father's overwhelming condition.	Despite using hyperbolic words like *profusely*, Josh's definition poem on page 154 accurately describes his father's overwhelming condition.	

Try incorporating evidence from "The Man Made of Words" using the following sentence frames:

- Momaday uses _____ to explain how stories have power. According to Momaday, _____, which supports the idea that _____.

- Momaday shows the power of stories when he states: _____.

- Momaday's use of words like _____ accurately describes his idea that _____.

Name _____

Date _____ Class _____

Handout 27A: Evidence Collection

Directions: *Review the informational texts in this module and consider your understanding about the power of storytelling across the three texts.*

	"Your Brain on Fiction," Annie Murphy Paul	"The Man Made of Words," N. Scott Momaday	"The Danger of a Single Story," Chimamanda Ngozi Adichie
What does this text say about the power of storytelling?			
Provide the two most effective pieces of textual evidence for your answer above.			

What's one idea about stories that connects these texts?

Handout 28A: Identify and Revise Sentence Structure

PART 1:

Directions: *Read the paragraph below. Underline simple sentences, circle compound sentences, and place a star at the start of complex sentences:*

¹Stories help readers better understand the world by allowing them to experience the adventures and conflicts of characters. ²In "Your Brain on Fiction," Annie Murphy Paul uses evidence from scientific studies to show how stories have power: ³"Words like 'lavender,' 'cinnamon' and 'soap,' for example, elicit a response not only from [. . .] but also those devoted to dealing with smells" (1). ⁴By making readers' brains respond as though they were experiencing the actual event, stories expose readers to new experiences without leaving their homes. ⁵Most importantly though, Paul shows the power of stories when she writes that stories let readers "identify with characters' longings and frustrations"(3) and hone "our real-life social skills" (3). ⁶Telling and reading stories can actually make people more considerate and socially aware. ⁷Storytelling is powerful because it lets writers and readers explore new parts of the world. ⁸Storytellers allow readers to gain better understanding of the lives of other people.

PART 2:

Directions: *With a partner, respond to the prompts below:*

- Revise sentence 4 to make the relationship between ideas clearer.

_____
_____
_____

- Read sentences 6–8 aloud to your partner. How does this portion of the paragraph sound?

_____
_____
_____

Name

Date   Class

- Revise sentences 6–8 to include variety in sentence structure.

Name _____

Date _____ Class _____

Handout 29A: EOM Poetry Portfolio Planning Packet

What does it mean to be a storyteller?

Directions: Use this packet to guide you through the process of planning, drafting and revising your poetry portfolio. Throughout the next five lessons, track your progress with this checklist:

Planning Packet Checklist	
Item	Completed?
Read Assessment 29: EOM Task	
Read and Annotate Handout 29B: EOM Exemplar Poems	
Complete Step One in packet	
Complete Step Two in packet	
Deconstruct Handout 30A: EOM Exemplar Cover Letter	
Complete Step Three in packet	
Complete Step Four in packet	
Complete first draft of my poetry portfolio	
Complete Step Five in packet	
Complete Step Six in packet	
Complete Step Seven in packet	
Revise my poetry portfolio	
Complete my cover letter	
Check my second draft using Handout 30C: Narrative Writing Checklist	
Complete my final draft	
Perform my poetry portfolio	

Name _____

Date _____ Class _____

Step One

Directions: *Brainstorm a list of experiences that shape you your sense of self and who you are—or that define your family. Try to think of an experience that took place over a shorter period of time than The Crossover—you will not have a whole novel to tell many months' worth of story! Brainstorm in the space below.*

Brainstorm Ideas:

- A time you witnessed something you knew was not right, and you did something about it;
- A time that you felt misunderstood, and how you responded to the misunderstanding;
- A time that you experienced a conflict with a family member or friend and were able to resolve it;
- A time you attempted something difficult, faced challenges, and learned from your experiences;
- A time of your choosing that feels significant to you!

Step Two

Directions: *After you have brainstormed your list of experiences, use the following flowchart to evaluate these ideas. Record at least two to three ideas that meet the criteria, as well as a few sentences about why you think they might work.*

Experience *Briefly describe the experience (e.g., the time I broke my sister's nose)*	Evaluate *Briefly record a few sentences about why this idea might work.* *Why is this experience important? What did you learn about yourself? How did it shape or change your sense of yourself or the world? What will others learn about you from reading about this experience?*

Name _____

Date _____ Class _____

Now you will need to decide which experience you want to focus on. Look over your list of experiences that meet the criteria: which are you most interested in writing about? Record your decision in the chart below.

I am writing about:	

Step Three

Directions: Taken together, your three poems will create a narrative arc. You will need to consider the order of events in your poems in more detail to give your reader a sense of the whole story. In order to make sure your narrative has meaning, as well as a narrative arc, you will also need to reflect on each moment you choose: why is it important?

Narrative Arc	Details What happened? What did you do? See? Smell? Hear? Feel?	Reflections What did you learn about who you are, what shapes your sense of yourself or the world, or where you've come from through reflecting on these events?
Beginning How did it begin? What's the first thing you remember?		
Middle What are the most important moments? Was there a point of tension or conflict? A turning point? If you told this story to a friend, what would they need to know to understand what happened?		
End How did it end? These events may still impact your life today, but telling a narrative means you have to end your story somewhere—what moment will you choose for an ending to your story?		

After you have decided on your plot points, find a partner and tell him or her your story out loud. Then reflect: Are there any details you included with your partner that you didn't include on your chart? Did you decide to describe a different moment to your partner? Was anything unclear? Edit the chart above as necessary.

Step Four

Directions: Next, you will need to decide which poetic type will best express the content and purpose of each poem; that is, the meaning you are trying to communicate. From the following list, choose a different poetic type for each of the three poems in your portfolio and consider how the type relates to your poem's content and purpose:

- A definition poem (e.g., "cross-o-ver" [29])

- A list poem (e.g., "Five Reasons I Have Locks" [14–15])

- An ode (e.g., "Ode to my Hair" [33])

- A time-stamp poem (e.g., "Game Time: 6:00pm" [125–127])

- A found materials poem (e.g., "Article #1 in the Daily News (December 14)" [155])

- An occasional poem (e.g., "Mom, since you asked, I'll tell you why I'm so angry" [204])

| Poem
Describe the content and meaning of each of your poems, and give each one a title. | Poetic Type
Choose from the list above. | Why
How does this type relate to your poem's meaning: its content and purpose? |
|---|---|---|
| Beginning | | |
| Middle | | |
| End | | |

Name _____

Date _____ Class _____

WAIT! Before you complete Step Five, make sure you have completed the following tasks:

- **Completed a first draft of my poetry portfolio.**
- **Read and annotated the exemplar cover letter.**

Step Five

Directions: *After you have completed the first draft of your poems and before you receive peer feedback, write a cover letter with three ToSEEC paragraphs (i.e., paragraphs each containing a **Topic Sentence**, **Evidence**, **Elaboration**, and a **Concluding Statement**) in which you:*

Provide the context of the story: • Consider your audience: what background information would help your reader understand your story? • Why was this a significant experience?	
Explain each poem in terms of the poetic type you chose: • Why is that poetic type the right choice for that poem? • How does the form of the poetic type relate to the content of the poem?	
Explain what you learned about the Essential Question of the module and what a reader might learn about the power of storytelling through this poetry portfolio: • Draw on one informational article from the module in order to consider the power of storytelling. • Apply your understanding of the power of storytelling to one poem in your portfolio. • What did you learn about yourself as a storyteller through this experience?	

Using these notes, independently compose a cover letter for your poetry portfolio.

Name

Date   Class

Step Six
Directions: *Based on your partner's feedback, and any feedback from your teacher, explain your plan for revision:*

I received the following feedback from my partner...

I received the following feedback from my teacher...

I plan to revise my poetry portfolio by...

Name _____

Date _____ Class _____

Step Seven

Directions: *Share your poetry portfolio with a partner. Your partner provides feedback here:*

Reviewed by: _____

These poems convey a clear narrative arc. The beginning is _____. The middle is _____. The end is _____.	Yes / No
These poems convey a deeper meaning. What I learned is _____ _____.	Yes / No
The forms of these poems match their content and meaning. The most effective form is _____ because _____.	Yes / No
These poems contain sensory, descriptive, and figurative language metaphors. The language is effective in the story because _____ _____. *Review list of criteria for effective descriptive and sensory language generated in Lesson 3.	Yes / No
What are the most effective aspects of your partner's poetry portfolio?	
How do the poetic types in the poetry portfolio impact your understanding of the story?	

Handout 29B: EOM Exemplar Poems

Directions: *Read the following exemplar poems.*

A One in a Million Chance
By Sara Clarke

Diagnosis

Friday, October 3rd, 3:15pm
Mom picks me up after school
I can tell she has been crying, **black rivers**
Streaking down her face.
We are both silent on the drive to the doctor's office.

Friday, October 3rd, 4:45pm
On the way home from the doctor
We both cry.

Tuesday, October 7th, 5:10am
I am so thirsty but they don't let you
Drink anything for 12 hours before surgery.
A week ago right now I was sleeping,
I was about to wake up and watch TV,
Eat my cereal, have a totally normal day.
Today is the new normal, I think, **as I get sleepy**
From the anesthetics.

Tuesday, October 21th, 7:30am
I am going back to school today. It doesn't
Seem real that two weeks ago I was on an
Operating table, a week before that
I didn't know any of this was real.
I have a big angry scar, **like the world's ugliest**
Necklace, hiding underneath my scarf.
I guess this is the new normal, even if
Nothing really feels normal anymore.

Report Card

English – A+
Math – A –
Social Studies – A
Science – A

Sara missed
two weeks of school
this semester
due to surgery.

She is a quiet student
she hasn't talked
about her illness and
she hasn't missed a beat.

Let Me Tell You How I Got This Scar

I got in a fight with a tiger, a dragon, and a really mean cat.
I went sky diving and got hit by lightning.
I got into a knife fight with pirates, and won.
I can't tell you where I hid the gold, though.I sang in an opera and hit the high C note.
It's just a cool new trend, I'm ahead of the curve.
I have magic powers, like Harry Potter.
Scar? What scar? I think you must be seeing things.
Actually, I had cancer and I beat it.
And no, I'm not contagious, and yes,
I'll have this scar forever.

And, yes, I am OK.
Thanks for asking.

Handout 30A: EOM Exemplar Cover Letter

Directions: *Read the following exemplar cover letter.*

A One in a Million Chance
By Sara Clarke

Cover Letter:

The fall after I turned fourteen my doctor found a lump on my throat. At first they thought it was just nothing, but they decided to check for thyroid cancer anyway. They told me there was only a one in one million chance that it was, but it turned out I was that one in a million! I was diagnosed, had surgery, and went back to school all in less than a month. In this series of poems, A *One in a Million Chance*, I explain the experience of going back to school after my surgery, feeling like the world was moving fast and slow at the same time, and realizing that I am capable of overcoming really difficult experiences.

The first poem, "Diagnosis," is a time-stamp poem. I chose a time-stamp structure because it allowed me to show exactly how quickly everything happened from the time I was diagnosed until I was back in school. The second poem, "Report Card," is a poem using found materials. This poem shows someone else's perspective on my situation and this time in my life, and it shows that even if I felt totally out of place and weird, that I was actually really brave and capable of being okay after my surgery. Finally, my third poem, "How I Got This Scar," is an occasional poem of all the responses I gave when people asked how I got my scar. This poem shows how humor helped me to be able to talk about what happened and helped me get back to a "new normal" after my experience.

These poems show the narrative of my illness and recovery, and also the growth I went through as a person because of this experience. I struggled with how emotional it was for me to write and share these poems—writing about personal issues is so difficult! Exploring the way that retelling difficult stories can help us process them, Benedict Carey explains: "Mental resilience relies in part on exactly this kind of autobiographical storytelling." This is particularly true in my first poem, "Diagnosis," because I had to think about my reactions to this illness step by step. Ultimately, telling my story in these poems helped me to better understand my own reactions to my diagnosis, and that is a powerful way stories can shape the way we understand ourselves.

Handout 30B: Drafting Cover Letter Paragraphs

Directions: *Outline and summarize each of the paragraphs from the exemplar cover letter on Handout 30A.*

Paragraph 1

Central Idea:
Supporting idea:
Supporting idea:
Summary:

Paragraph 2

Central Idea:
Supporting idea:
Supporting idea:
Summary:

Paragraph 3

Central Idea:
Supporting idea:
Supporting idea:
Summary:

Name _____

Date _____ Class _____

Handout 30C: Narrative Writing Checklist

Directions: *Self-assess your EOM Task, then give the checklist to a peer and your teacher.*

Narrative Writing Checklist	Self +/ Δ	Peer +/ Δ	Teacher +/ Δ
Reading Comprehension			
I use three distinct poetic types.			
I provide background information about my story in my cover letter.			
I explain the relationship between each poetic type and the content of the poem in my cover letter.			
I apply an understanding of and incorporate evidence from one informational article in my cover letter.			
I reflect on what I learned about myself as a storyteller in my cover letter.			
Structure			
I respond to all parts of the prompt.			
I establish a context for my narrative.			
I organize my events according to a narrative arc.			
My conclusion follows from the events, providing resolution.			
Development			
I write about an experience that is significant to me.			
I use description to develop events and experiences.			
I use descriptive details.			
I use sensory language.			
I use at least one to two examples of figurative language (metaphor, simile, hyperbole).			
Style			
I use a variety of sentence patterns (simple, compound, complex, compound-complex) to add clarity and interest to my cover letter.			
I use precise words and phrases to describe what happened.			
My writing style is appropriate for the audience.			
I consider oral expression when writing.			

Name: _____

Date: _____ Class: _____

Conventions			
I use commas, ellipses, and/or dashes to add clarity to my writing.			
I use indicative, imperative, and/or interrogative verb moods to convey my thoughts and feelings.			
Writing Process			
I prewrite and brainstorm before writing my portfolio.			
I outline the narrative arc of the poetry portfolio.			
I consider the best poetic structures that relate to the meaning of my story.			
I revise after receiving feedback from my partner and my teacher.			
Total # of checks			

Volume of Reading Reflection Questions
The Poetics and Power of Storytelling, Grade 8, Module 1

Student Name: _____

Text: _____

Author: _____

Topic: _____
_____

Genre/type of book: _____

Directions: Share your insights about your independent reading text by answering the questions below.

1. Wonder: What drew your attention to this text? What qualities about the story or the structure enticed you to read it?

2. Wonder: How will reading a text in this structure be different than a traditional narrative?

3. Organize: Describe the way that the author organized the narrative. How is the experience of reading a narrative written in verse different than a more traditional narrative structure?

4. Organize: What examples from this text highlight the author's central themes?

5. Reveal: How do specific language and structural choices of the author convey and/or develop a theme?

6. Distill: How does this text deal with storytelling, and the idea that storytelling shapes the way people think about themselves and the world?

7. Distill: How does the author's decision to write this book as in a non-traditional structure, such as a novel-in-verse, support the themes in the book?

Name

Date   Class

8. Know: In what ways has studying different narrative structures, such as novels-in-verse, and learning about storytelling contributed to your enjoyment of this text?

9. Know: Does reading this book encourage you to seek out more novels written in verse? Explain.

WIT & WISDOM PARENT TIP SHEET

WHAT IS MY EIGHTH GRADE STUDENT LEARNING IN MODULE 1?

Wit & Wisdom is our English curriculum. It builds knowledge of key topics in history, science, and literature through the study of excellent texts. By reading and responding to stories and nonfiction texts, we will build knowledge of the following topics:

Module 1: The Poetics and Power of Storytelling

Module 2: The Great War

Module 3: What Is Love?

Module 4: Teens as Change Agents

In this first module, The Poetics and Power of Storytelling, students will study how we build community, understand ourselves, and explain the world around us using stories and poems. They will read a novel and poetry and ask the question: What is the power of storytelling?

OUR CLASS WILL READ THESE TEXTS:

Novel

- The Crossover, Kwame Alexander

Articles

- "This Is Your Life (and How You Tell It)," Benedict Carey
- "Your Brain on Fiction," Annie Murphy Paul, The New York Times

Poetry

- "Nikki-Rosa," Nikki Giovanni
- "Slam, Dunk, & Hook," Yusef Komunyakaa
- "Sometimes Silence Is the Loudest Kind of Noise," Bassey Ikpi

Speech

- "The Danger of a Single Story," Chimamanda Ngozi Adichie

Music

- "Filthy McNasty," Horace Silver

OUR CLASS WILL EXAMINE THESE WORKS OF ART:

- *The Block*, Romare Bearden
- *Children's Games*, Pieter Bruegel the Elder

OUR CLASS WILL WATCH THESE VIDEOS:

- "Sometimes Silence Is the Loudest Kind of Noise," Bassey Ikpi
- "Nikki Rosa on Def Jam Poetry," Nikki Giovanni
- "Slam, Dunk, & Hook," Yusef Komunyakaa
- "The Danger of a Single Story," Chimamanda Ngozi Adichie
- "The Human Soul Distilled," Reading Rockets

OUR CLASS WILL ASK THESE QUESTIONS:

- What shapes Josh Bell's sense of himself and his world?
- How does form shape a story's meaning?
- What is the role of expression in storytelling?
- How do stories help us make sense of ourselves and the world?
- What does it mean to be a storyteller?

QUESTIONS TO ASK AT HOME

As your eighth grade student reads, ask:

- *What do you notice and wonder?*

BOOKS TO READ AT HOME:

- *Spoon River Anthology*, Edgar Lee Masters
- *I Am Phoenix*, Paul Fleischman
- *Inside Out and Back Again*, Thanhha Lai
- *Brown Girl Dreaming*, Jacqueline Woodson
- *Witness*, Karen Hesse
- *The Red Pencil*, Andrea Davis Pinkney

IDEAS FOR DISCUSSING THE POWER OF STORYTELLING:

You can talk about storytelling at any time, anywhere. Ask:

- *What's your favorite family story? Why?*
- *Tell me a story you remember from your childhood.*
- *Share a story with your eighth grader about your childhood.*

CREDITS

Great Minds® has made every effort to obtain permission for the reprinting of all copyrighted material. If any owner of copyrighted material is not acknowledged herein, please contact Great Minds® for proper acknowledgment in all future editions and reprints of this module.

- All material from the *Common Core State Standards for English Language Arts & Literacy in History/Social Studies, Science, and Technical Subjects* © Copyright 2010 National Governors Association Center for Best Practices and Council of Chief State School Officers. All rights reserved.
- All images are used under license from Shutterstock.com unless otherwise noted.
- For updated credit information, please visit http://witeng.link/credits.

ACKNOWLEDGMENTS

Great Minds® Staff

The following writers, editors, reviewers, and support staff contributed to the development of this curriculum.

Ann Brigham, Lauren Chapalee, Sara Clarke, Emily Climer, Lorraine Griffith, Emily Gula, Sarah Henchey, Trish Huerster, Stephanie Kane-Mainier, Lior Klirs, Liz Manolis, Andrea Minich, Lynne Munson, Marya Myers, Rachel Rooney, Aaron Schifrin, Danielle Shylit, Rachel Stack, Sarah Turnage, Michelle Warner, Amy Wierzbicki, Margaret Wilson, and Sarah Woodard.

Colleagues and Contributors

We are grateful for the many educators, writers, and subject-matter experts who made this program possible.

David Abel, Robin Agurkis, Elizabeth Bailey, Julianne Barto, Amy Benjamin, Andrew Biemiller, Charlotte Boucher, Sheila Byrd-Carmichael, Jessica Carloni, Eric Carey, Janine Cody, Rebecca Cohen, Elaine Collins, Tequila Cornelious, Beverly Davis, Matt Davis, Thomas Easterling, Jeanette Edelstein, Kristy Ellis, Moira Clarkin Evans, Charles Fischer, Marty Gephart, Kath Gibbs, Natalie Goldstein, Christina Gonzalez, Mamie Goodson, Nora Graham, Lindsay Griffith, Brenna Haffner, Joanna Hawkins, Elizabeth Haydel, Steve Hettleman, Cara Hoppe, Ashley Hymel, Carol Jago, Jennifer Johnson, Mason Judy, Gail Kearns, Shelly Knupp, Sarah Kushner, Shannon Last, Suzanne Lauchaire, Diana Leddy, David Liben, Farren Liben, Jennifer Marin, Susannah Maynard, Cathy McGath, Emily McKean, Jane Miller, Rebecca Moore, Cathy Newton, Turi Nilsson, Julie Norris, Galemarie Ola, Michelle Palmieri, Meredith Phillips, Shilpa Raman, Tonya Romayne, Emmet Rosenfeld, Jennifer Ruppel, Mike Russoniello, Deborah Samley, Casey Schultz, Renee Simpson, Rebecca Sklepovich, Amelia Swabb, Kim Taylor, Vicki Taylor, Melissa Thomson, Lindsay Tomlinson, Melissa Vail, Keenan Walsh, Julia Wasson, Lynn Welch, Yvonne Guerrero Welch, Emily Whyte, Lynn Woods, and Rachel Zindler.

Early Adopters

The following early adopters provided invaluable insight and guidance for Wit & Wisdom:

- Bourbonnais School District 53 • Bourbonnais, IL
- Coney Island Prep Middle School • Brooklyn, NY
- Gate City Charter School for the Arts • Merrimack, NH
- Hebrew Academy for Special Children • Brooklyn, NY
- Paris Independent Schools • Paris, KY
- Saydel Community School District • Saydel, IA
- Strive Collegiate Academy • Nashville, TN
- Valiente College Preparatory Charter School • South Gate, CA
- Voyageur Academy • Detroit, MI

Design Direction provided by Alton Creative, Inc.

Project management support, production design, and copyediting services provided by ScribeConcepts.com

Copyediting services provided by Fine Lines Editing

Product management support provided by Sandhill Consulting